W9-AMO-306

Published by Smart Apple Media
1980 Lookout Drive, North Mankato, Minnesota 56003
Produced by Byron Preiss Visual Publications, Inc.

Cover design by Dean Motter
Interior design by Gilda Hannah
Edited by Howard Zimmerman

Front cover art by Mark Hallett
Back cover art by Patrick O'Brien

Art Credits: Pages 1, 16 © 2002 Mark Hallett. Pages 3, 23 © 2002 Patrick O'Brien.
Pages 5, 7, 26, 27 © 2002 Phil Wilson. Pages 9, 10–11, 17, 28–29 © 2002 Douglas
Henderson. Page 12 © 2002 John Sibbick. Page 13 © 2002 Berislav Krzic. Page 21
© 2002 Rich Penney. Page 31 © 2002 Joe Tucciarone.

Printed in the U.S.A.

Library of Congress Cataloging-in-Publication Data

Olshevsky, George.
Triceratops / by George Olshevsky and Sandy Fritz.
p. cm.—(Discovering dinosaurs)
Summary: Presents information on *Triceratops*, including physical
characteristics, diet, habitat, known social organization, close relatives,
and areas where fossils have been found.
ISBN 1-58340-178-4
1. Triceratops—Juvenile literature. [1. Triceratops. 2. Dinosaurs.]
I. Fritz, Sandy. II. Title.
QE862.O65 O478 2002
567.915'8—dc21   2002017636

First Edition

2 4 6 8 9 7 5 3 1

TRICERATOPS

Sandy Fritz and George Olshevsky

SMART APPLE MEDIA

inosaurs lived on Earth from about 227 million to 65 million years ago. Scientists call this the Mesozoic era. It is also called the Age of Reptiles or the Age of Dinosaurs. Dinosaurs were closely related to today's reptiles and birds. In fact, many scientists now think that birds evolved from a small meat-eating dinosaur that was a swift runner. All dinosaurs were land animals. Flying reptiles (called pterosaurs) and reptiles that swam in the sea also lived during this period, but they were not dinosaurs.

The Age of Dinosaurs, the Mesozoic era, is divided into three periods. The earliest period is called the Triassic, which lasted from 248 million to 205 million years ago. Dinosaurs first appeared around the middle of this period. The Jurassic period followed, lasting from 205 million to 145 million years ago. The final period is called the Cretaceous. The Cretaceous spanned from 145 million to 65 million years ago. After the Cretaceous, dinosaurs were gone.

But during their time, dinosaurs lived everywhere on Earth, even in Antarctica. About 700 different kinds of dinosaurs have been unearthed, and many more remain in the ground awaiting discovery. There were meat-eating dinosaurs that could run fast on their long hind legs. There were four-legged, plant-eating dinosaurs 150 feet (46 m) long and weighing as much as 100 tons (91 t)! There were dinosaurs with horns, crests, and bony armor. Some dinosaurs, both meat-eaters and plant-eaters, were as small as chickens or house cats.

Everything we know about dinosaurs comes from fossils that people have dug up from the ground. Scientists examine, measure, and analyze these fossils. From them we can learn when and where dinosaurs lived. We have learned how dinosaurs walked and ran, what they hunted, and what plants they ate. We can even figure out how long they lived. Presented in this series is the most up-to-date information we have learned about dinosaurs. We hope you'll enjoy reading all about the fabulous beasts of Earth's distant past.

Meet Triceratops

The three-horned face and tank-like stance of *Triceratops* makes it one of the most recognizable of dinosaurs. It first appeared about 72 million years ago, during the Cretaceous period. *Triceratops* lived alongside other dinosaur groups, such as tyrannosaurs, hadrosaurs, ankylosaurs, sauropods, and "dome-headed" dinosaurs.

Triceratops was an herbivore, a plant-eating animal. When full grown, it could weigh as much as three to four tons (2.7–3.6 t). This is about the same weight as a modern elephant. But it was far longer than an elephant, growing to about 30 feet (9 m) long. *Triceratops*'s huge head, curved horns, and bony neck frill were

When scientists first began to study dinosaurs, they compared them to living reptiles such as crocodiles and alligators. So, many of the early discoveries were thought to have lived in watery, swampy areas. Now we know dinosaurs were more like birds and mammals in many ways than they were like reptiles.

features shared by most of its relatives. This group of dinosaurs is called the ceratopsids.

Most *Triceratops* fossils have been found in river delta deposits, where rivers once drained into the sea. This could mean *Triceratops* lived near rivers, but it could also be misleading. The dinosaurs may have died some distance away, and had their bones washed into the river by heavy rains and floods. Scientists think *Triceratops* lived on dry land rather than in a marshy area such as a river delta.

The Cretaceous World

A sudden and important change swept over the world 140 million years ago, at the beginning of the Cretaceous period. This was when flowering plants appeared. At first, flowering plants grew only on hills and mountains. But by the end of the Cretaceous, they had become the world's most common kinds of plants.

Triceratops belonged to the dinosaur group called ceratopsians. They first appear in the fossil record at the same time as the first flowering plants. The new environment in the Cretaceous probably favored new kinds of dinosaurs. The fossil record shows more types of dinosaurs lived then than in any earlier time. Towering trees still

During the Cretaceous, the continents continued to drift further apart. The Rocky Mountains and the European Alps began to form at this time. The narrow sea that would become the Atlantic Ocean continued to spread and deepen.

A *Triceratops* in search of food walks along the shoreline of an ancient stream.

existed, but new trees and plant life were appearing. These new plants had different kinds of leaves and tough bark. Some had flowers. *Triceratops* was nicely adapted to eat the new plants.

Many trees and shrubs that are familiar to us existed in the late Cretaceous. Oak, hickory, and magnolia trees took root at that time. Laurel and barberry shrubs appeared. In swampy areas, cypress and giant sequoias towered over turtles, frogs, birds, and a host of dinosaurs.

Discovering Triceratops

Traces of horned dinosaurs have been found in the American West since 1855. But the early finds were just bone fragments and teeth. Slowly, the clues began to build up. Two fossil horns were discovered near Denver, Colorado, in 1877. They were first identified as horns from an extinct bison. Then, in 1889, a complete *Triceratops* fossil skull with similar horns was found in Wyoming. It wasn't until 1899 that all the pieces of the puzzle came together. All the finds belonged to a massive, plant-eating dinosaur. It was *Triceratops*.

Triceratops roamed what is now western North America. Its fossils have been found in Colorado, Wyoming, South Dakota, Alberta, and Saskatchewan. More than 100 fossil skulls and other remains of *Triceratops* have been uncovered so far. (Since full

A couple of male *Triceratops* vie for the top spot in the herd, while a group of *Struthiomimus* (birdlike dinosaurs) runs past in the foreground.

Above: Ceratopsians. From left to right: *Triceratops*, *Pachyrhinosaurus*, **and** *Styracosaurus*. **Opposite page:** *Torosaurus* **(right) had a larger frill than its cousin** *Triceratops*.

fossil skeletons are rare, many museum displays are made from the pieces of different fossils.)

As more and more fossil finds appeared, scientists divided *Triceratops* into 16 different species. But recent work has shown that there were only two species of *Triceratops*. One species, *Triceratops prorsus*, had straight horns above the eyes and a large nose horn. The other, *Triceratops horridus*, usually had curved horns above the eyes and a small nose horn.

Triceratops means "three-horned face" in Greek. All the ceratopsian relatives of *Triceratops* featured horns. These horns were ridges of bone that grew above the animal's eyebrows and on the tops of their snouts. Each species sported a different arrangement of horns. *Centrosaurus* had a long, central nose horn but only tiny brow horns. Six spikes bristled from the neck frill of *Styracosaurus*. *Torosaurus* sported brow horns longer than hockey sticks. *Einiosaurus* had just one horn on its nose that drooped forward.

All ceratopsids shared a similar design. The hind legs of *Triceratops* and other ceratopsids were longer than their front legs. This probably helped them graze on ground plants without having to use too much energy, since it placed the head closer to the ground.

The frills of most ceratopsids had holes in them to keep them light. These holes were covered by skin. *Triceratops* is the exception. Its frill was made of solid bone, but was very thin.

Understanding the Fossils

Triceratops, like many early dinosaur discoveries, was first portrayed with its legs splayed out to the sides. This is because early researchers used crocodiles as models for their reconstructions. By the early 1980s, scientists knew that dinosaurs did not look and move like reptiles. The image of *Triceratops* changed to one closer to a rhinoceros. It was pictured as an animal that stood and walked on four straight legs. But scientists still weren't sure. Now, new work done at the Smithsonian Institution may have answered the question.

After dismantling the Smithsonian's *Triceratops* for repairs, scientists scanned images of its fossil skeleton into a computer. From the scans, full-sized replicas of the bones were made. They also made a model (about the size of a dog) and tried out different postures. It seems that *Triceratops* didn't stand like a rhino or a lizard. Its hind legs were held straight—but its front legs were slightly splayed out to the sides.

Arrhinoceratops was a close cousin of Triceratops. Here, a pair of them move through a barren area in search of low-lying plant food.

The posture meant that *Triceratops* was not a fast-running animal like a rhino or a bison. Instead, it was built for sturdiness. If attacked, *Triceratops* probably dug in and fought rather than attempting to run away. After all, it did have some dangerous weapons with which to defend itself. The two horns above *Triceratops*'s eyes grew to more than three feet (1 m) long. The horns were better protection than the large neck frill.

The bony neck frill of *Triceratops* is a feature found only among neoceratopsid dinosaurs. This is the specific subgroup of frilled and horned dinosaurs of which *Triceratops* was the largest member. The frill is actually an extension of the back of the dinosaur's skull. Scientists think that the frill's main function was to anchor the animal's massive jaw muscles. The long stretch of the muscles from the frill to the jaw would have given *Triceratops* incredible chewing power. Although it appears to shield the animal's neck, the frill was too thin to be a good defense. It might have been used for temperature control. Lots of blood vessels in the frill could have cooled *Triceratops*'s blood, the same way that blood vessels in an elephant's big ears help keep it cool.

Many scientists believe *Triceratops*'s frill was probably a colorful display. The frill may have been patterned or colored in a way that

**Above: A group of *Triceratops* forms a defensive circle around several youngsters. They are being circled by a pair of *Tyrannosaurus rex*, who are trying to get to the babies.
Opposite page: Another cousin of *Triceratops* was *Styracosaurus*. This painting shows the ceratopsians with the correct stance: front legs bowed a bit to the sides, rear legs firmly under the body for support.**

was different for each of the ceratopsids. That would have helped them find each other. When alarmed or angered, *Triceratops*'s frill may have become flushed with color. This would have made it appear bigger, tougher, and meaner.

The Eating Machine

*T*riceratops bit off plant food with its beak. The bony edges formed a sharp slicing surface. The animal must have used the beak to bite off branches and leaves with a powerful snap. Once plant food was inside *Triceratops*'s mouth, it was worked on by an impressive set of teeth. Hundreds of teeth filled *Triceratops*'s jaws. They were constantly replaced during its lifetime. As old teeth wore down, new ones took their place. The top and bottom teeth fit together like the blades of a pair of scissors.

Slicing up the food was done with an up-and-down movement rather than a sideways chew. The scissors-like teeth sliced the food into smaller pieces rather than mashing it. After a *Triceratops* swallowed, the food was probably moved into chambers called gizzards. Here the food was ground up with the help of gizzard stones. These stones, called gastroliths, were swallowed by the animal to help grind up its food.

This view of the legs of *Triceratops* was considered the correct reconstruction until recently. Now we know that the dinosaur's front legs bowed out to the sides when it walked.

Triceratops spent many hours a day filling its large stomach. Imagine how much plant food a whole herd of Triceratops could have eaten in a single day. We have good evidence that ceratopsids lived in herds. Vast fossil bone beds of dinosaurs related to Triceratops have been found in Montana and Canada. The fossil remains of adult and young ceratopsids were found mixed together. One bone bed looks like an entire herd may have been wiped out suddenly, possibly in a raging flood.

A herd of 30-foot-long (9 m) horned dinosaurs may have behaved like some modern herding animals. They would have slowly traveled across the land that held their favorite plants, eating as they went. Triceratops was a grazing animal. It ate plants that grew low to the ground. Members of the herd could walk slowly and eat a fresh meal as they went.

Being part of a herd helped to protect each dinosaur, especially the babies and other young ones. If a predator or two attacked, the herd of adults could chase them away. But a young Triceratops, all alone, might become their next meal.

If Triceratops lived in herds it also would have traveled in herds. And sometimes these travels would have been for many days, covering hundreds of miles.

Triceratops Migrations

In the modern world, animals migrate as food becomes scarce. They also migrate to return to breeding grounds to have their babies. Triceratops and its kin may have migrated for the same reasons.

During the time when Triceratops lived, an inland sea

Two male *Triceratops* lock horns in an attempt to prove who should be the leader of the herd. These duels could cause injuries, but they were usually not fights to the death.

divided North America. Along the western edge of this sea, many dinosaur trackways have been found. (Trackways are footprints that have turned to stone.) Running north and south, they record the movement of many types of dinosaurs. Most of the tracks come from plant-eating dinosaurs, which were generally large and heavy. Some of the trackways have been identified as belonging to either *Triceratops* or one of its cousins.

Tracks by themselves aren't proof that dinosaurs such as *Triceratops* migrated. Other clues can be found in fossil bone beds. Bone beds of ceratopsid dinosaurs have been found from Alaska to Texas. They include the fossils of both adult and young dinosaurs. Sometimes the groups had hundreds of individuals.

Scientists think the bone beds, along with the trackways, show that *Triceratops* and other plant-eaters were migrating animals.

Triceratops the Fighter

The horns of *Triceratops* weren't just for show. No predator would have wanted to attack this plant-eater head-on. But there is evidence that *Triceratops* locked horns with others of its own kind. Puncture holes found in *Triceratops* face bones seem to show that they fought with each other.

Modern animals that butt heads do so to see which member of the herd will become the leader. But because of their large size, *Triceratops* may have only locked horns and shoved each other

A group of *Triceratops* moves through the North American West during the dry season. They have found a small water hole, but must be wary of predators.

around, rather than smashing into each other the way bighorn sheep do. Bighorn sheep have a space in their skull below the horns that helps cushion the shock of impact. A similar feature has been found in *Triceratops*. A hollow space near the root of its brow horns helped cushion the head from the shock of impact.

Healed rib fractures are also found in *Triceratops* fossils. These injuries appear between the hip and the mid-flank. American bison display the same type of injury. In bison, the injury is caused by one animal using its head to butt another in the side. The same behavior may have caused similar injuries in *Triceratops*. So the evidence seems to show that *Triceratops* fought with each other. But they also had to defend themselves from predators.

One famous predator shared the same time and space with *Triceratops*. It was *Tyrannosaurus rex*, the "king tyrant lizard." Weighing in at seven tons (6.5 t), *T. rex* was heavier than an elephant, and stretched more than 40 feet (14 m) long when fully grown. Some scientists think *T. rex* was too big and heavy to be an effective hunter. This may be so. An adult *T. rex* may simply have dined on the kills of other predators after chasing the predators away. But younger, smaller, faster tyrannosaurs probably

Other evidence exists that *T. rex* fed on *Triceratops* and its cousins. A *T. rex* coprolite (fossilized dung) was found to have pieces of bone in it from the neck frill of a young ceratopsid.

A pair of young *Tyrannosaurus* spook a herd of *Triceratops*. They hope to isolate one of the slower, older plant-eaters from the rest.

hunted, chased, and killed their own meals. Some of those would have been the occasional *Triceratops*.

Many *Triceratops* fossil bones have been found with *T. rex* bite marks. One fossil *Triceratops* bone was discovered with 58 separate *T. rex* bite marks. But some scientists think it was too dangerous for *T. rex* to attack a healthy, full-grown *Triceratops*. Its horns could inflict serious injuries. A crippling wound would have prevented a predator

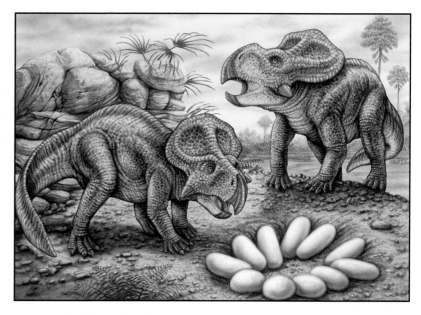

from hunting and killing its prey. It was probably only the very young, the very old, or the injured *Triceratops* that became a meal for *T. rex*.

Triceratops Young

No known *Triceratops* eggs have yet been found. But like all dinosaurs, they must have laid eggs. It's possible that the male and the female *Triceratops* were different sizes. This is the case with *Protoceratops*, an early relative of *Triceratops* that lived in Mongolia. Dozens of intact fossil skeletons of *Protoceratops* have been unearthed there. Adults seem to fall into two general sizes, with one size bigger than the other. It's possible that the larger adults were the males. In modern herding animals, the male is frequently larger than the female. This may also have been true for *Triceratops* and its relatives.

This page and opposite: There is fossil evidence that *Protoceratops* mothers protected their nests and took care of their babies until they could feed themselves. Scientists think *Triceratops* did the same.

A herd of *Triceratops* migrates to their nesting ground as a *Tyrannosaurus* watches carefully. If one of the plant-eaters should fail the river crossing, it will become the meat-eater's next meal.

But the largest difference between the male and the female *Protoceratops* was the frill size. Whichever sex was larger had larger frills as well. This trait may have also applied to *Triceratops*.

Fossil bone beds have allowed scientists to study how ceratopsids grew. There are many samples of young and adult animals. Scientists found that at least three ceratopsids closely related to *Triceratops* looked identical when they were young. Only when they became full-grown did the horns appear. The display of horns may have signaled that the animal was old enough to mate.

The End of an Era

Ceratopsids were among the last groups of dinosaurs to appear, and among the last to vanish. Ceratopsids were successful in the late Cretaceous world because they had good equipment to eat the new plants that had taken over. It's no coincidence that as flowering plants appeared, *Triceratops* and its relatives became the dominant plant-eaters of the time. And then they became extinct.

Most scientists think that the end of the Age of Dinosaurs was a sudden event. It may have been the result of a mountain-sized meteorite smashing into the earth. This would have caused fires to rage across the entire world and filled the air with dust and ashes for many, many years. Some scientists also think that the changing climate, the changing plant life, disease, and gases released by volcanic explosions contributed to the death of the dinosaurs.

Dinosaurs were not the only group of animals to disappear at that time. Other victims included many families of fish, snails, sponges, birds, and mammals. On land, as much as 85 percent of all animal species became extinct.

An old *Triceratops* bull is ambushed by a pair of *T. rex*. But they'd better eat fast because their world is about to end. A meteorite as big as a mountain is about to smash into the earth, ending the Age of Dinosaurs.

GLOSSARY

ankylosaurs (an-KIE-luh-sawrz): group of plant-eating armored dinosaurs with low, barrel-shaped bodies.

Arrhinoceratops (a-RIEN-o-SER-a-tops): a close cousin of *Triceratops*. A ceratopsian dinosaur.

Centrosaurus (SEN-tro-SAWR-us): a relative of *Triceratops* with a long, central horn but only tiny brow horns.

ceratopsian (ser-uh-TOP-see-un): a group of four-legged dinosaurs with short tails, huge heads, and a bony frill covering the neck.

Einiosaurus (ie-nee-uh-SAWR-us): a ceratopsian relative of *Triceratops* with a small horn on its nose that drooped forward.

extinct (ik-STINKT): no longer existing.

fossil (FAH-sill): a remnant of a living organism that has turned to stone over time.

frill (fril): an extension from the back of the head that covers the neck.

gastroliths (GAS-tro-liths): stones swallowed by plant-eaters to help break up their food.

gizzards (GIZ-urdz): pockets of the stomach in which food is broken down for digestion.

grazing (GRAY-zing): eating grass or plants that are low to the ground.

hadrosaurs (HAD-ruh-sawrz): the "duck-billed" dinosaurs.

herbivore (URB-uh-vor): any plant-eating animal.

Pachyrhinosaurus (pak-ee-RIEN-o-SAWR-us): a ceratopsian dinosaur with thickened bones in place where the nasal horn is usually found.

predator (PRED-uh-tor): an animal that hunts and eats other animals for food.

Protoceratops (PRO-tuh-SER-uh-tops): an ancestor of the *Triceratops*.

pterosaurs (TERR-uh-sawrz): flying reptiles from the Mesozoic era.

Struthiomimus (STROOTH-ee-uh-MIME-us): birdlike dinosaurs.

Styracosaurus (STIR-uh-ko-SAWR-us): a ceratopsian with six long spikes on its frill plate.

Torosaurus (TORE-uh-SAWR-us): a ceratopsian with brow horns over three feet (1 m) long.

trackways (TRAK-wayz): footprints left in the mud that have changed to stone over a long time.

Triceratops (try-SER-uh-tops): a ceratopsid dinosaur with a three-horned face, powerful beaked jaws, and a short, bony frill.

Triceratops horridus (try-SER-uh-tops hor-RID-us): one of two species of *Triceratops*. This species was identified by the curved horns above the eyes and a small nose horn.

Triceratops prorsus (try-SER-uh-tops PROR-sus): one of two species of *Triceratops*. This species was identified by the straight horns above its eyes and a large nose horn.

tyrannosaurs (tie-RAN-uh-sawrz): group of two-legged, meat-eating dinosaurs.

Tyrannosaurus rex (tie-RAN-uh-SAWR-us REX): a tyrannosaurid. One of the largest meat-eaters that ever lived.